# UNIQUE
# ORIGIN
## OF ALL
# 31 NHL TEAM
## NAMES, LOGOS
## AND COLORS

### TOM WATERS

AuthorHouse™
1663 Liberty Drive
Bloomington, IN 47403
www.authorhouse.com
Phone: 833-262-8899

Because of the dynamic nature of the Internet, any web addresses or links contained in this book may have changed since publication and may no longer be valid. The views expressed in this work are solely those of the author and do not necessarily reflect the views of the publisher, and the publisher hereby disclaims any responsibility for them.

Any people depicted in stock imagery provided by Getty Images are models, and such images are being used for illustrative purposes only.
Certain stock imagery © Getty Images.

This book is printed on acid-free paper.

ISBN: 978-1-6655-2236-6 (sc)
ISBN: 978-1-6655-2237-3 (e)

Library of Congress Control Number: 2021907312

Print information available on the last page.

Published by AuthorHouse  01/17/2022

**author**HOUSE®

This is a short report of how every team in the National Hockey League got its name, logo and club colors. We focus on how unique each of the 31 teams' names, logos and colors are without comparing each to the others. We also try to point out how the teams uniquely reflect the city or locale where they play. Many of these team names, logos and colors also refer to folk legends, untamed animals, military connections, social issues at the time or were just developed through word of mouth. The primary color of most teams is clearly known but not all the secondary colors. Some of these teams have used other logos and sets of colors in the past but this report focuses mainly on the present. Each team is listed according to how long they have played in their present location. The year they each started play there is listed to the right of the team name.

# MONTREAL CANADIENS 1917

The name, logo and colors are based on Canadian society from that era. This team has a French name since it originally represented the French speaking (francophone) population of Montreal which is why the name is spelled in French. Their popular nickname, "Habs", is an abbreviation of the word Habitants, the name referring to the early settlers of New France; now modern day Quebec.

Their colors, red, white and royal blue are patterned after the Union Jack and the Red Ensign, two flags commonly flown in Canada at the time.

The logo stands for both the French and English translation of Canadiens Hockey Club.

What is so unique about this team's name, logo and colors is they have gone the longest of any team in the league without changing them.

The Montreal Canadiens became the team of the entire city in 1938 after the collapse of the old Montreal Maroons who represented English speaking (anglophone) Montreal at the time.

# TORONTO MAPLE LEAFS 1917

It was not till after their first decade of NHL play that the present name and colors were adopted. They were both suggested by the legendary Conn Smythe who had just purchased the team. Mr. Smythe had served in the recently fought First World War with a Canadian army unit called the Maple Leaf Regiment. The members of this unit wore a brass maple leaf on their army helmets.

The colors blue and white represent the winter weather. Conn Smythe was reported as saying "with hockey being an outdoor game, blue represents the sky, white the snow".

The present logo was designed in 2016 to honor the team's 100th anniversary of NHL play. There are 31 points around the edge of the leaf commemorating 1931, the most memorable or legendary year in that team's history. That is the year they opened their former legendary arena, Maple Leaf Gardens. Also the 17 veins represent the period of 1917 to 2017, the year they started playing in the NHL to the year they celebrated their 100th anniversary in the league. Thirteen of those 17 are on the top portion of the leaf representing the number of Stanley Cups they have won.

# BOSTON BRUINS 1924

Boston was the first US city admitted into the National Hockey League. The team founder, Charles F. Adams, was a grocery tycoon based in Boston. The colors were chosen first, the name second, present logo third and finally the shoulder patch.

Brown and yellow were the business colors of Mr. Adams grocery chain. He wanted to name the team after an untamed animal commonly brown in color. An organization member suggested the name Bruins, an old English word referring to brown bears in classic folk tales. The color brown was changed to black in 1934.

The primary logo featuring a letter B placed in the center of a wheel signifies the city's nickname "The Hub of New England". A 19th century Boston area author, Oliver Wendell Holmes, described Boston as the hub of the universe. A logo featuring the letter B was introduced in 1948 to celebrate the team's 25th anniversary but the present design was introduced in 2008.

The secondary logo, introduced in 2007, is worn on the shoulders of the jersey. It is almost like a reversed design of the original Bruins logo from 1924. The road jersey has Boston printed above and Bruins below while the home jersey has it the other way around.

# NEW YORK RANGERS 1926

After the city of New York completed its first year of NHL play with a team called the Americans it was thought there were enough people and interest to support an additional team and form a local rivalry (Big Apple mentality and unique for New York City).

The Rangers were named after the state police of Texas and one would wonder what that has to do with New York. One of the team's partners was a native Texan, George (Tex) Rickard, president and promoter of events for New York City's legendary arena Madison Square Garden. While promoting this brand new team, the other partners and local newspapers jokingly called them Tex's Rangers. Ironically this nickname stuck.

The Rangers' colors blue, red and white are the same as the old New York Americans but the Rangers have always denied copying from them. The team logo, designed like a crest or shield, was to look similar to the New York Americans' logo. One major difference was that the Americans spelled their name horizontally on their logo while the Rangers chose to spell theirs diagonally.

The Rangers became the Big Apple's sole NHL team following the demise of the New York Americans in 1942.

# CHICAGO BLACKHAWKS 1926

This is the only major league sport team named after a Native American icon, Chief Black Hawk. He was the leader of an American aboriginal tribe who played a major part in the War of 1812. Later in life he went on to contribute quite significantly to the history of Illinois and become a real legend there.

But the team was actually named after a US army unit bearing Chief Black Hawk's name. The team founder, Frederick McLaughlin, served with that unit in the First World War. He was also operating a dining business in Chicago called the Black Hawk restaurant.

The origin of the colors red, black and white are not clearly known but believed to have a military connection.

The present uniform and main logo were designed in 1954 despite a few minor changes made since then. This particular logo features Chief Black Hawk with war paint on his face bearing the team colors.

The team sweater features a piece of hockey memorabilia believed to be a first. The Blackhawks are believed to be the first major league hockey team to introduce a shoulder patch. It was not till three or four decades later, 1980's and early 90's, that other teams, amateur and professional, started to adopt this kind of patch.

The two words, Black and Hawks, were amalgamated in 1986 to form the single word Blackhawks. This was because of a discovery at that time in the original franchise documents.

# DETROIT RED WINGS 1926

This team went by two other names before adopting its present name in the early 1930's. They had just been purchased by James Norris, a Detroit businessman originally from Montreal.

The colors red and white were already in place under the two previous names (Cougars and Falcons). But Mr. Norris' plan was to keep the original colors and introduce a new name and logo.

One of the most unusual things about this team is that the logo was adopted before the team name was chosen. Mr. Norris took this logo from an amateur hockey team in Montreal he had played for called the Winged Wheelers. They were part of the Montreal Amateur Athletic Association (MAAA). He thought a wheel in the logo seemed ideal for Detroit's prominence in the emerging automobile industry. But he still had to redesign the present logo for copyright reasons.

After matching the new logo with the team colors he came up with the brilliant idea of naming his team the Red Wings.

# PHILADELPHIA FLYERS 1967

The name 'Flyer' has little to do with the city of Philadelphia. It was one of the most popular of three or four names voted in by local fans. The original general manager, Bud Poile (father to Nashville GM David Poile), once managed a minor pro team in Edmonton called the Flyers. He managed to convince the team founder to adopt that as the team name. It was also confirmed that majority owner Ed Snider liked that name because of his special fondness for ice skating shows. "Flyers" also referred to people skating and sliding around the ice.

The colors orange and white were thought of by minority owner William Putnam. They were the colors of his alma mater, the University of Texas. As well when none of the original six teams had orange among their colors. Black was adopted to pay special honor to the color worn by an earlier NHL team in Philadelphia called the Quakers who existed only in the 1930-31 season.

The logo was designed by a local artist. It features a stylized letter P shaped as a hockey stick along with a set of wings representing speed and is known as the "Winged P". The orange circle depicts a hockey puck (despite orange not being the true color of a puck).

# PITTSBURGH PENGUINS 1967

People would wonder why the city of Pittsburgh would name a team after a flightless bird found only in Antarctica? However, "Penguins" was one of over 700 of 26,000 contest entries and also because the first three letters can be abbreviated for Pittsburgh, Pennsylvania. Another reason was because the exterior of the city's original arena was shaped like an igloo. This gave local fans the idea of penguins playing in an igloo even though those birds live in Antarctica. Also, an igloo is a traditional Inuit shelter found in northern Canada and Alaska and not in Antarctica.

The logo features a penguin skating through the Golden Triangle, a geographic landmark based on how the three rivers come together in Pittsburgh. The Golden Triangle also makes up the city's central business district.

Black and gold became the team colors in 1980. They are the colors of the city's two other major league teams; the Pirates of major league baseball and the Steelers of the National Football League. The Pirates and Steelers won a total of six championships in the 1970's. It was thought the colors of the city's two recent championship winners would help sell the team to the public. Black and gold also reflect the city's prominence in the steel industry.

# ST. LOUIS BLUES 1967

The name "St. Louis Blues" was originally a song written by a jazz musician, William C. Handy, in the early 1900's, so the city has a history of jazz and blues music. Despite this name being copyrighted the team founders, Sid Soloman Jr. and Sid Soloman III, chose it because they wanted a name that would sell to the public. Luckily they successfully adopted this name without facing legal action.

The team name tried to stay with the musical theme of "the blues". This dictated the choice of blue being the team's dominant color.

A musical note was chosen as the logo to continue this connection. The Blues logo is also believed to have a hidden meaning. That winged note bears a striking resemblance to what's known as the 64th note on the musical scale. It could also have some bearing on the fact that the city of St. Louis was founded in 1764. This has never been confirmed as fact but was a popular theory among local fans. The darker shade of navy blue was added in 1998 to compliment the lighter blue.

# LOS ANGELES KINGS 1967

The team founder was Jack Kent Cooke, a Canadian who moved to Los Angeles. He chose the name Kings for reasons he never made public. One theory however, is the city had a hockey team in the 1930's called the Monarchs who played in the old Pacific Coast Hockey League.

The present colors black, silver and white were adopted in 1988, the year NHL superstar Wayne Gretzky landed with the team. These were the same colors as one of the city's major league football teams, the old Los Angeles Raiders who later moved back to their original home in Oakland. They were worn until the mid-1990's and reclaimed in 2008. The reason for reclaiming these colors was because they were worn during the team's most successful years along with paying special honor to Gretzky.

The primary logo can be considered a shield or coat of arms bearing a royal or medieval appearance. With Los Angeles being regarded as one of the largest cities or possibly the largest in the world known more by its initials then its actual name, it was thought that it would be wise for that to stand out extra clear in the logo. The crown at the bottom displays a pair of hockey sticks and sunspots signifying hockey played in a hot sunny climate.

# BUFFALO SABRES 1970

This team was started up by two brothers, Seymour and Northrup Knox, both Buffalo businessmen. They decided the buffalo would be on the logo regardless of what the team would be named. They wanted a name referring to leadership, superiority or a high ranking. This gave them the idea to choose the name Sabres out of a contest because of it being a weapon carried by a leader and considered a symbol for authority. When you compare that to any team sport or battle between combatants a sabre includes both a position of offense or defense. With the Knoxes being involved in the game of polo, they were intrigued by names connected to cavalry, knighthood and chivalry.

The Knox brothers chose navy blue and gold for the team colors patterned after a local polo club where they had family connections.

The Sabres adopted a new logo and colors in 1996. This was because of moving into a new building and the change was meant to celebrate the dawn of a new era. After trying three different logos and sets of uniforms for nearly a decade and a half, they went back to their original dress wear in 2010. When the original logo was reclaimed the colors navy blue and yellow were darkened to look more bright and the color silver was added.

# VANCOUVER CANUCKS 1970

The fictional character, Johnny Canuck, has been portrayed in a specific role that has fan appeal in Vancouver and the entire province of British Columbia. This features him as a toque wearing lumberjack and hockey player in his spare time.

The team colors blue, green and white are the original colors but the Canucks have not worn them continuously. They wore another set of colors and different logo for nearly 30 years. A change of ownership in 2006 decided to reclaim the original uniforms but adopt a brand new logo. Blue represents the Pacific Ocean, green the forests of BC, and white the snowcapped mountains.

The main logo is a letter C designed to look like an aboriginal art craft native to the province, likely the Haida tribe. The top half features an orca killer whale leaping out of the icy waters of the ocean, one of the most recognizable creatures found in the Pacific. It also represents the name of the current owner, Orca Bay and Sports Entertainment.

The original logo is now worn as a shoulder patch. This features a letter C designed to look like an ice surface with a hockey stick jutting out of it.

# NEW YORK ISLANDERS 1972

This team represents Long Island, a suburb of New York City. With the team playing on a piece of land completely surrounded by water it was only evident that the team name should somehow incorporate the idea of an island. Originally the name "Long Island Islanders" was considered but it was decided this would sound awkward. So the wife of the team founder, Roy Boe, suggested calling them the New York Islanders. This was meant to attract unhappy Ranger fans whose team had gone far too long since last winning the Stanley Cup.

They chose a set of colors they thought would appeal to the public. Blue and orange were the colors of two other major league teams in the Big Apple, Knicks (NBA) and Mets (MLB) as well these were the colors of the county of Nassau where the team began play.

The logo features a map of Long Island surrounded by the state initials and team name. The letter Y for New York is shaped like a hockey stick with a puck alongside. There were originally three stripes on the Y shaped stick but a fourth was added in 2008 to commemorate the four Stanley Cups won by this team. The top of the letter I in Islanders points to exactly where on the island the team plays.

# WASHINGTON CAPITALS 1974

The name Capitals was chosen by a contest to reflect the nature of Washington DC. Their colors red, white and navy blue are based on the tricolored US flag. The stars and stripe figure on their sweaters are patterned on both the US flag and the flag of Washington DC.

This team wore two other uniform colors and logos from 1995 to 2007 but then they went back to a revised version of the original uniforms as well as a revision of the original logo. The letter t in Capitals is shaped like a hockey stick with a red puck alongside. The three stars above the name Washington are based on the local flag. Those three stars each represent the three separate primary geographic areas that circle around the city of Washington; the states of Maryland, Virginia and the District of Columbia.

The shoulder patch is the American bald eagle shaped as a W. An outline bearing the dome of the US Capitol building can be seen underneath, designed to be very American.

# EDMONTON OILERS 1979

This team originally played in a league called the World Hockey Association (WHA) from 1972 to 1979. They were founded by Bill Hunter, a prominent Canadian entrepreneur.

He chose the name Oilers out of a contest since it represented the most prominent industry of Alberta. They were originally called the Alberta Oilers. But a year later they changed their name to represent just the city of Edmonton as the oil capital of Canada.

The top of the team logo displays a drop of oil looking almost like a flame. The letters of Oilers appear to be sitting in a pool of oil meant to represent the present while the design underneath is the oil underground representing the future. This team's logo has the strongest reference to a present and future meaning than any other team logo in the league.

The choice of the colors blue, orange and white are not clear. But Mr. Hunter also owned a junior team in Edmonton called the Oil Kings who wore blue, red and white. This team wore orange as the dominant color on their jerseys when starting out in the old WHA but later changed blue to the dominant color. Those original orange sweaters were reclaimed in 2015 to be worn as an alternate uniform. But in 2017 they became the main one due to fan popularity.

# CALGARY FLAMES 1980

The city of Calgary moved a team from Atlanta, Georgia already called the Flames. They were originally planning to change the team name to something that would reflect the western heritage of Calgary and held a team naming contest. But to the surprise of many people most fans voted to retain the name Flames. This was likely because they were tired of more traditional names and felt the name Flames seemed ideal for an oil town.

This meant they would keep the same uniform and colors brought from Atlanta; red, yellow and white. The only change was redesigning the logo from a flaming A to a flaming C. Although several years later the original flaming A was restored to signify the team's alternate captains. The color black was added in 1995 because of the color's popularity of the 1990's which resulted in the original uniform having to be redesigned.

This would further result in the Flames trying several different jersey designs over the next 20 years. But the present jersey, permanently adopted in 2017, was introduced in 2007. It features the Alberta and Canadian flags on the players' right and left shoulders respectively as a means of showing provincial pride. This making them the only Canadian team wearing its provincial and national flags on their jerseys.

# NEW JERSEY DEVILS 1982

Reference to the devil has a non-religious folk history in New Jersey and is part of local state folklore. For about the last two or three centuries people in this US state have been telling stories about an evil mythological creature called the Jersey Devil. This fictitious character is believed to roam around the Pine Barrens of southern New Jersey destroying agricultural crops, killing livestock and doing physical harm to man. The Jersey Devil originated from sorcery or some kind of witchcraft and became the official state demon in 1939.

The Jersey Devil is to New Jersey what the Loch Ness Monster is to Scotland and to what Ogopogo is to the Okanagan region of British Columbia.

Because of the team name it was obvious that red would be the dominant color. Green was originally a secondary color but in 1992 it was changed to black because of the color's popularity of that decade. The logo features the state initials joined together with the top of the letter J bearing devil's horns and the bottom being a long pointed tail against the background of a puck.

# SAN JOSE SHARKS 1991

The team was named after the most feared sea animal found along the California coast; especially in an inlet in the Bay Area called the Red Triangle. There are also several shark research facilities along that triangle.

Although the Sharks represent the entire Bay Area of Northern California, the team name represents San Jose because of the arena being there.

The colors Pacific teal, burnt orange, black and white are based on the view of the Pacific Ocean off the California coast.

The logo features a shark chomping on a hockey stick by leaping out of what is believed to be the triangular figure (trifecta) of the three major cities in the Bay Area; San Jose (south), San Francisco (west), and Oakland (east).

The present shoulder patch was introduced in 2017 featuring an angry looking shark as a means of showing aggressiveness and excitement.

# OTTAWA SENATORS 1992

The Senators returned to the NHL following an absence of nearly 60 years. When the city was readmitted into the league, fans voted to reclaim the original name. This was because the original Senators won 11 Stanley Cups and local fans thought it would be great to get reconnected with its successful past. The present team is thought of as the reincarnated Ottawa Senators.

The team name obviously stands for the political prominence of the city but one would wonder how this applies to the team logo. The team founder wanted the logo to stand for aggressiveness and excitement so that is why they chose an old Roman senator to dominate the logo's appearance. The present logo has been redesigned from the original in 1992. It features the head of a Roman general who would have served as a member of the Roman Republic's senate.

The original Senators wore green, red and white colors. But because of the color novelty of the 1990's green was changed to black with gold being added.

The shoulder patch bearing the capital letter O is the logo worn by the original Senators during their last five years in existence_ 1929-1934.

# TAMPA BAY LIGHTNING 1992

The original founders included brothers Phil and Tony Esposito, two retired NHL superstars who had both taken permanent residence in Tampa Bay. Phil also served as the team's first general manager. It was through him the team would receive their name by way of unusual circumstances. He was reported to have been inspired by a local major lightning storm that gave him the idea of this name. With Tampa Bay bearing status as the lightning capital of North America such a name would seem a perfect fit. Phil was also reported to have stated that "lightning represents the quick pace of a hockey game, as well as a common sight in the Tampa skies".

Royal blue, black, silver and white were chosen for the team's colors; a unique combination for any team in the league at the time. A change of ownership in 2011 decided to change the team colors and sweaters to a more traditional design and retain blue and white as the main colors. Silver was dropped while black is now just a trim color for the numbers.

It was appropriate for a lightning bolt to appear on the logo. The present logo is a redesigned version of several logos this team has had in the past. It features a lightning bolt on the background of a puck.

# DALLAS STARS 1993

The City of Dallas, Texas brought in the team from Minnesota called the North Stars. With Texas known as the Lone Star State it was obvious that keeping the second half of the original name was a perfect fit for Dallas. This enabled them to keep the same uniforms (black trimmed with green, yellow and white) and logo worn in Minnesota. The only minor change was adding a shoulder patch bearing a map of Texas.

A brand new owner in 2013, Thomas Gagliardi, decided to give the team a new identity by changing the colors and introducing a new logo that was more unique and appealing for the city of Dallas. After consulting local fans, it was thought that green should become the primary color in order to make the Stars more recognizable among all 30 teams. So Victory green was chosen for the new primary color, the same shade of green worn by the old NHL team Hartford Whalers. However, the original yellow did not mix with Victory green so they reluctantly changed it to silver.

The present logo design is known as the ninja star, featuring the team name (Stars) and city's nickname (the Big D) blended together. That star and letter D are sharply designed to look like a spur; an ideal fit for the state of Texas.

The shoulder patch bearing the map of Texas was transferred from the shoulder to the team pants when new uniforms were unveiled in 2013.

# ANAHEIM DUCKS 1993

This team was originally named the Anaheim Mighty Ducks by the team founder Walt Disney Productions. They named it after a popular movie about hockey recently released called 'Land of the Mighty Ducks'. A change in ownership in 2006 thought it best to give this team a new identity. The new owners, Henry & Susan Samueli, dropped the word Mighty and just kept Ducks as the team name because most of their season ticket holders requested that.

Following the change in name a new set of colors were introduced; black, gold, orange, silver and white; the suitable colors of a real duck. The orange color is also believed to be a metaphorical link to the name of the location in California where Anaheim is situated- Orange County.

The main logo is the letter D shaped as the webbed foot of a duck. The secondary logo featuring a 1970's goalie mask with two hockey sticks crossed together was originally the main logo when known as the Mighty Ducks. Following the name change it was reclaimed as the shoulder patch to meet of fan pressure. The Ducks wear black as the dominant color on the main jersey and orange the dominant one on the alternate jersey.

# FLORIDA PANTHERS 1993

The Florida panther is a breed of the North American cougar living in the forests and swamps (Everglades) of Florida. This creature has also become an endangered species. So most local hockey fans voted this name in to help increase widespread exposure and generate efforts to save this endangered native wildcat of Florida.

The team colors red, navy blue, yellow-gold were taken from the state flag of Florida as a means of appealing to the local public.

The present logo and shoulder patch were adopted in 2016. The new majority owner, Vincent Viola, wanted the Panthers to appear as if they were heading into a new era. He wanted the main logo to center around boldness, courage and sacrifice. So he patterned the new logo after a military unit he once served with in the United States army called the '101st Airborne Division'. One obvious change was placing a panther on the original design of that old military logo. The home jerseys read Panthers on the main logo while the road jerseys read Florida.

The shoulder patch features a crawling panther overtop of a redesigned version of the state flag. One minor change on the state flag features the state seal being removed and replaced with a blazing sun signifying the Sunshine state. The top of that patch reads Florida at home and Panthers on the road.

# COLORADO AVALANCHE 1995

This team was transferred in from Quebec City after being purchased by COMSAT Entertainment Group, based in Denver. COMSAT gave local fans eight names to choose from. The majority chose Avalanche because of the Rocky Mountains in Colorado being prone to these events.

They kept the blue and red colors from Quebec but chose red to be the dominant one. The original blue and red were changed to different shades- steel blue and burgundy red. They also added black and silver as a means of developing a color combination unique for any team in the league, a novelty of the 1990's.

The logo features a mountain shaped as the letter A on the background of a puck. This mountain is designed with a falling avalanche led by another puck forming the letter C.

That logo worn on the shoulder was adopted in 2015 to celebrate the team's 20th anniversary in Colorado. It features an insignia from the state flag bearing the team colors.

# ARIZONA COYOTES 1996

The Coyotes originally represented the city of Phoenix but changed their name to represent Arizona in 2014 to try and increase statewide interest. The majority of fans voted in this name because of it being the most common predator roaming through the southwest desert region of that state. For years Phoenix had a hockey team called the Road Runners playing at the minor pro level and briefly in the old WHA. This created a widespread belief that fans also thought of the name because of the old Bugs Bunny cartoon featuring a coyote trying to capture a road runner with no success.

The Coyotes have worn their present uniforms since 2003. Their colors are brick red, desert sand, black and white, a color combo appearing ideal for a team playing in a desert.

The main logo is based on traditional Navajo artwork displaying a coyote howling at the moon. Those four triangles on the coyote's fancy nose represent the Four Peaks, a mountain landmark of four snow covered peaks visible from the Phoenix metro area.

Unlike any other NHL team, the Coyotes wear separate shoulder patches on their home and road jerseys. The home jersey features a paw print of a coyote forming a letter A form within. The jersey worn on the road displays a map of Arizona included with a partial design of the state flag and the state's abbreviation.

# CAROLINA HURRICANES 1997

The Hurricanes were named after the coastal storms that frequently devastate the local area. The team plays in the city of Raleigh, North Carolina but represent both states of North and South Carolina. When the Hurricanes learned they were to share their new arena with the North Carolina State University (NCSU) basketball team they decided to adopt the NCSU colors of red, black and white. This was a means of selling their product mainly to people in Raleigh and the surrounding area. But they also added the color silver.

The logo features somewhat of a bird's eye view of a puck caught in a fast moving hurricane. In meteorological terms it looks almost like a symbol for a hurricane. It has been dubbed as the 'Eye of the Hurricane' logo.

The Hurricanes adopted a new logo for a predominantly black color alternate jersey adopted in 2018. It displays two hurricane warning flags joined together in such a way to form a map of North Carolina. This is meant to show regional pride.

# NASHVILLE PREDATORS 1998

This is the second NHL team in history to adopt their logo before the name. The logo is based on discovering the fossil remains of a prehistoric saber tooth tiger found buried underground in downtown Nashville in August 1971, by a construction crew doing an excavation. A very bizarre incident remembered by the local populace to this day.

The name Predators was later chosen out of a contest based on the logo, a suitable name for a team hoping to live by defeating other teams.

The original colors were a unique combination of navy blue, orange, gold, silver and white. But in 2011 orange and silver were dropped. Gold became the primary color which was unique for any team in the league.

The present uniforms were also unveiled in 2011 and show a set of fangs in the neck area. Because of Nashville known as Music City USA these uniforms are also musically designed. A total of six guitar strings are sketched in the back numbers along with piano keys designed inside the collar.

The secondary logo, a guitar pick inserted with three stars is worn on the shoulders. The former refers to the city's musical heritage while the latter represents the state flag of Tennessee.14 Those three stars refer to the state's three grand divisions; West, Middle and East Tennessee.

# MINNESOTA WILD 2000

This team was named after a combination of the natural rugged wilderness of Minnesota, local wildlife and the outdoor scenery of that US state in general.

The entire color scheme centers around the outdoor landscape of Minnesota; Forest green, Iron range red, Harvest gold, white for the snow along with the color of wheat. Green was originally the primary color but in 2003 an alternate jersey with red as the main color was adopted and became the permanent jersey in 2007. However, Minnesota once had a team in the league called the North Stars who wore green as the primary color. Hockey fans were sentimental about that color so Forest green was reclaimed as the main color in 2017.

The logo features a wild animal commonly found in Minnesota with the late night scene of a forest inside the face. People may interpret that animal as either a bear, badger or timber wolf but there is really no definite answer to that question. That animal's mouth resembles a stream of water, the eye a star and the ear a full moon. The actual star is shaped like the North Star which is their way of paying tribute to the old Minnesota North Stars.

The design of the letter M worn as a shoulder patch was introduced at the 2016 outdoor Stadium game. It became a fan favorite and has since become a popular symbol for promoting Wild hockey.

# COLUMBUS BLUE JACKETS 2000

Blue Jackets is the nickname of the uniforms worn by the Union (Yankee) Army in the US Civil War. The team name pays honor to the pride and patriotism shown by citizens of Ohio during that war. Both the state of Ohio and city of Columbus contributed greatly to the Union Army. Ohio sent more soldiers to the Civil War than any other US state. Four notable Union Army leaders also came from Ohio; Ulysses Grant (future US president), William Sherman, Philip Sheridan and George Custer. The city of Columbus contributed by manufacturing a large portion of Union Army uniforms (blue jackets).

The primary logo features a stylized version of the Ohio state flag wrapped around a silver star forming the letter C. That star signifies Columbus as the state capital of Ohio. Their colors union blue, red, silver and white are based on that very flag.

The present jersey was introduced as an alternate jersey on Columbus Day (October 13, 2003) and wound up becoming the primary one in 2007.

That cannon logo is worn as a shoulder patch. It is designed to look like the type of cannon commonly fired during the Civil War.

# WINNIPEG JETS 2011

The original Winnipeg Jets were named for the city's growth in the Canadian airline industry, especially when Winnipeg was becoming a central transferring point for Canadian airline passengers. But they still had to receive approval from the New York Jets of the National Football League for use of the name. When the city of Winnipeg got readmitted into the NHL after a 15-year absence the majority of fans voted to retain the original name.

The two logos are patterned after the Royal Canadian Air Force (RCAF) which had just come back into being after a 40+year absence and the city has an air base known as 17 Wing Winnipeg. Both logos still needed approval from the Canadian Defense department. The primary logo is a redesigned version of the RCAF roundel. That jet plane was added by the team and is a design of an RCAF fighter jet known as the McDonnell Douglas CF-18 Hornet. The notch in the blue circle indicates the jet flying northward. That is in reference to the name of the team's owner, True North Sports & Entertainment.

The secondary logo is a hockey like version of an RCAF captain's wings and includes the Canadian maple leaf.

The team's colors are also of significance to the newly reincarnated RCAF; polar night (navy) blue with aviator blue, silver and white.

# VEGAS GOLDEN KNIGHTS 2017

The first half of the team's name centers around the state of Nevada being the largest producer of gold of any US state. While the second half is typifying the team as a group of warriors. One other reason for the name Knights is in reference to team founder Bill Foley's alma mater, the West Point Academy Black Knights.

The primary logo features the helmet of a medieval knight with a letter V for Vegas. But the shoulder patch bears a starburst design with two swords resembling a sign commonly seen in Las Vegas. This is the sign one can see when driving into the city from any direction; "Welcome to Fabulous Las Vegas".

The colors steel gray, gold, red and black are unique for any team in the league. Gray and black are centered mainly around strength, durability, power and intensity. Gold and red reflect the geographical outline of the Las Vegas area; gold for the terrain and red for the red rock canyons.

# SEATTLE KRAKEN 2021

# CONCLUSION

Many of these teams will probably make further changes to their colors, logos and other parts of their uniform. This project will continually be updated as time goes by.

# FOOTNOTES

1   The Name Game, Michael Leo Donovan, McGraw-Hill Ryerson Limited, 1996.
2   Wikipedia, the free encyclopedia (online).
3   The Calgary Sun, January 24, 1988, Lance Hornby.
4   The Globe and Mail, February 3, 2016, James Mirtle.
5   What's in a Name? by Rob MacNeil, Sportsnet Staff, September 17, 2010 (online).
6   BTLNHL/Hockey by design (online).
7   Bleacher Report, by Joe Gill, correspondent, April 3, 2011 (online).
8   The Hockey News logo rankings, Adam Proteau, August 5, 2014 (online).
9   Flyers History: How the Team was Named (online).
10  Origin of NHL Nicknames, Last Word on Sports, by Michael Kovacs, April 16, 2013 (online).
11  Gonna Fly Now: The Story Behind the Philadelphia Flyers Brand (online).
12  25 Things Hiding in Sports Logos, Mental Floss, by Rebecca O'Connell, July 13, 2015.
13  Guest Post: Worst to First Jerseys, St. Louis Blues Edition.
14  Sports Teams Logo History (online).
15  A Look at how NHL Teams got their team nicknames, by Eliot Kleinberg, Palm Beach Post Staff Writer, July 26, 2010 (online).
16  Canucks Wardrobe: A History from Hideous to Splendour (online).
17  Free Spirit Gallery (online).
18  Men of Teal: The Story Behind the San Jose Sharks, by Paul Caputo, October 25, 2014 (online).
19  Chris Creamer's Sportslogos.net, est. 1997.
20  Jerseys and Logos-Senators History Timeline-20 years of memories. A century of history (online).
21  Team Names origin.com.
22  James Mirtle. It's official: They're the Anaheim Ducks-a hockey journalist's blog; Friday, January 27, 2006 (online).
23  The Ducks Look-Anaheim Ducks (online).
24  Florida Panthers team owners interview; Vincent Viola, John Viola, Douglas Cifu (online).
25  Breaking Down the New Duds, part 2 (online).
26  Avalanche making changes for 20th season-icethetics (online).
27  Arizona Coyotes (1996)-Present-The Sports E-cyclopedia.
28  Nashville Predators Team History (online).
29  Nashville Predators Jersey History-The Hockey Writers (online).
30  Minnesota Wild/2017 Jersey Launch/Minnesota Wild-NHL.com.
31  Naming a Team: The Story Behind the Columbus Blue Jackets-Official website of the Columbus Blue Jackets.
32  Columbus Blue Jackets Unveil New Third Jersey (online).
33  True North Unveils Jets Logos, July 22, 2011 (online).
34  Vegas Golden Knights unveil name, logo and colors/The Hockey News (online).

# BIBLIOGRAPHY

1 A look at How NHL Teams got their team nicknames, by Eliot Kleinberg, Palm Beach Post Staff Writer, July 29, 2010 (online).

2 Arizona Coyotes (1996)-Present-The Sports E-cyclopedia.

3 Avalanche making changes for 20th season-icethetics (online).

4 Bleacher Report, by Joe Gill, correspondent, April 3, 2011 (online).

5 Breaking Down the New Duds, part 2 (online).

6 BTLNHL/Hockey by design (online).

7 Canucks Wardrobe: A History from Hideous to Splendour (online).

8 Chris Creamer's Sportslogos.net, est. 1997.

9 Naming a Team: The Story Behind the Columbus Blue Jackets-Official website of the Columbus Blue Jackets.

10 Florida Panthers team owners interview: Vincent Viola, John Viola, Douglas Cifu (online).

11 Flyers History: How the Team was Named (online).

12 Free Spirit Gallery (online).

13 Gonna Fly Now: The Story Behind the Philadelphia Flyers Brand (online).

14 Guest Post: Worst to First Jerseys, St. Louis Blue Edition.

15 James Mirtle: It's official: They're the Anaheim Ducks-a hockey journalist's blog; Friday, January 27, 2006 (online).

16 Jerseys and Logos-Senators History Timeline-20 years of memories. A century of history (online).

17 Men of Teal: The Story Behind the San Jose Sharks, by Paul Caputo, October 25, 2014 (online).

18 Minnesota Wild/2017 Jersey Launch/Minnesota Wild-NHL.com.

19 Naming a Team: The Story Behind the Columbus Blue Jackets-Official website of the Columbus Blue Jackets.

20 Nashville Predators Jersey History-The Hockey Writers (online).

21 Nashville Predators Team History (online).

22 Origin of NHL Nicknames, Last Word on Sports, by Michael Kovacs, April 16, 2013 (online).

23 Sports Teams Logo History (online).

24 Team Names Origin.com.

25 The Calgary Sun, January 24, 1988, Lance Hornby.

26 The Ducks Look-Anaheim Ducks (online).

27 The Globe and Mail, February 3, 2016, James Mirtle.

28 The Hockey News logo rankings, Adam Proteau, August 5, 2014 (online).

29 The Name Game, Michael Leo Donovan, McGraw-Hill Ryerson Limited, 1996.

30 True North Unveil Jets Logos, July 22, 2011 (online).

31 25 Things Hiding in Sports Logos, Mental Floss, by Rebecca O'Connell, July 13, 2015 (online).

32 Vegas Golden Knights unveil name, logo and colors/The Hockey News (online).

33 What's in a Name?, by Rob MacNeil, Sportsnet Staff, September 17, 2010 (online).

34 Wikipedia, the free encyclopedia (online).

Printed in the United States
by Baker & Taylor Publisher Services